Disney · PIXAR

FINDING DORY

THE ESSENTIAL GUIDE

Written by Glenn Dakin

CONTENTS

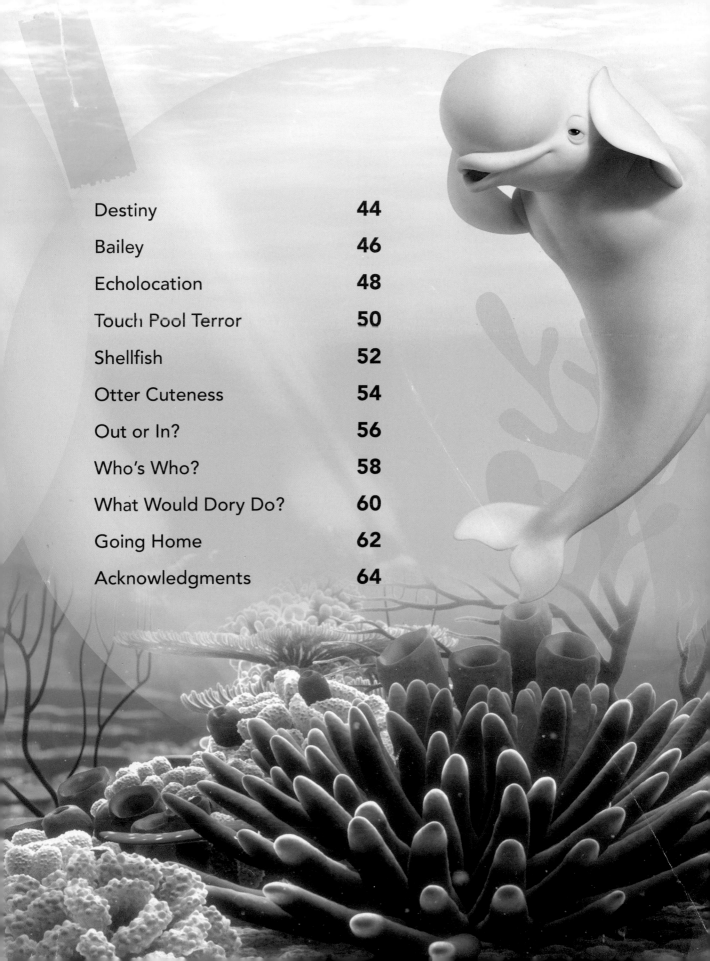

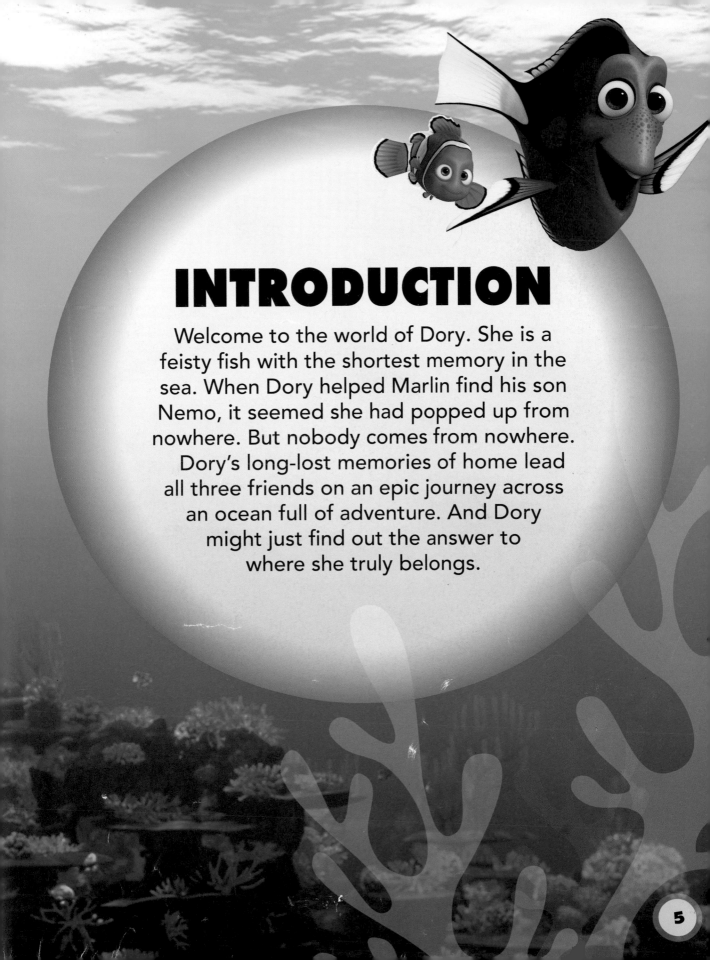

INTRODUCTION

Welcome to the world of Dory. She is a feisty fish with the shortest memory in the sea. When Dory helped Marlin find his son Nemo, it seemed she had popped up from nowhere. But nobody comes from nowhere. Dory's long-lost memories of home lead all three friends on an epic journey across an ocean full of adventure. And Dory might just find out the answer to where she truly belongs.

DORY

This bubbly blue tang makes friends everywhere she goes. The trouble is, Dory suffers from short-term memory loss so she often forgets sea creatures as soon as she meets them. Dory loves helping others, but one day she remembers her own problem—she has lost her family!

In and out of trouble

Dory's positivity helps her make the best of difficult situations. Even being caught in a plastic ring works to her advantage by bringing her closer to finding her family.

TRUE OR FISHY?

The blue tang is an extremely rare fish.

Fishy: It is not endangered and is found in many places.

New family

To find her folks, Dory needs the help of Nemo and Marlin— two clownfish who have become her new family.

"I HAVE A FAMILY!"

Eyes have wide range of vision

Pipe peril

Dory is forced to brave the pipe system of the Marine Life Institute (MLI) alone, but soon discovers that friends—and help—are never too far away.

Yellow tips on pectoral fins

DID YOU KNOW?

Talented Dory can speak whale and she can read, too!

Accepting herself

Dory gets frustrated with herself for being forgetful and needing others. It takes her a long time to realize that other fish appreciate her and need her, too.

JENNY AND CHARLIE

Dory's doting parents would do anything for her, but what they do most is worry about her memory. They teach her games and songs to help her remember and stay safe... But their biggest fear comes true when she goes missing.

Body is round and quite flat

Charlie

A dedicated dad, Charlie teaches Dory that when problems seem impossible to solve, there is always another way, if you keep on trying. He loves playing with his daughter, and calls her his little kelpcake.

Shell paths

After Dory goes missing, her parents spend years making paths of shells. They hope that one day she will find one to follow all the way back home.

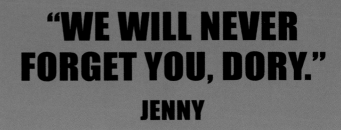
DID YOU KNOW?

Tangs really do like to live in pairs, just like Dory's mom and dad.

Flat, yellow tail

Body color can change from light blue to dark blue or purple

Jenny

Always cheerful in front of Dory, Jenny secretly worries that her daughter will struggle on her own. She warns Dory that she must always stay away from the undertow—the strong current that could pull her away from them.

Reunited

Jenny and Charlie always knew that Dory was special. However, they are still amazed to hear about all the adventures she has had and all the friends she has made.

9

Memory Guide

Having a memory with more holes in it than a fishing net can be a problem. Even remembering your way home can be hard! Luckily for Dory, her parents have come up with a helpful way for her to remember how to find her way home.

START

Are you lost?

Yes →

Uh oh! Go to the start and try again.

No

Remember what a shell trail looks like?

Yes

No

Remember what blue tangs look like?
(Hint: Just like you!)

Yes

No

Remember the "Just Keep Swimming" song?

No

Yes

Phew! Swim along home!

As a child, Dory is simply too small to be noticed by some of the fish she asks for help.

DID YOU KNOW?

Young tangs like Dory grow up feeding on teeny-tiny plankton. As tangs become older they add squishy green algae plants to their diet. Yum.

BABY DORY

TEEN DORY

LOST AT SEA

Separated from her parents, Dory grows up from a tiny tang to a full-grown fish. She roams the ocean all on her own, in search of her mom and dad. Every day she meets more new faces, until finally she finds another family who come to treat her like one of their own.

Still growing up, Dory bumps into a giant sunfish, who tells her to watch where she's going.

As a young adult, Dory finds that other sea creatures are often far too busy to help her, like these crabs.

GROWN-UP DORY

As a teen, Dory gets bolder and will chat to anyone, including swordfish, hoping for a clue to help her.

Grown-up Dory meets these sea urchins, but by now she doesn't even remember what she's looking for.

Dory is an adult when she crashes into Marlin and helps him find his son, Nemo. After that, this trio is as tight-knit as fish can get.

THE REEF

The beautiful coral reef is the perfect spot for a delightful residence. Here everyone knows their neighbor, and rarely eats them! Dory has her own cozy coral cave, and her clownfish friends dwell in the fronds of a nearby anemone.

400 different coral types live on the reef

Anemone with stinging fronds

Mind the sting!

A soft anemone swaying in the sea may look harmless, but only clownfish are welcome inside. All other fish who touch those fronds receive a nasty shock, as Dory regularly discovers!

TRUE OR FISHY?

Coral needs only sunlight and water to survive.

Fishy! It actually feeds on tiny plankton and fish.

14

Drop-off

The edge of the reef is known as the Drop-off. It is where the coral canyons end and the big ocean begins. Beyond it, anything can happen!

Organ pipe coral

Brain coral

Sleep talking

Dory never stops talking when she's awake—so it's no surprise that she talks in her sleep! Marlin and Nemo have learnt to tune out her sleep chatter.

MARLIN

Proud father Marlin is one of the biggest worriers in the sea and he can't stop giving out safety tips. He is dedicated to bringing up his son Nemo, and also to being there for Dory. Deep down, he is incredibly brave—once he crossed the ocean to find his lost son.

Meeting Dory

It was a life-changing moment for Marlin when he first met Dory. She helped him to find Nemo and she taught him to never give up.

DID YOU KNOW?

Clownfish are also known as anemone fish because they can live inside the venomous creature.

Powerful tail called a caudal fin

Dory dilemma

Marlin is worried about traveling across the ocean to find Dory's family. He'd much rather stay in their safe home!

No clowning around

One of the problems with being a clownfish is people expect you to be funny. Marlin is not good at telling jokes and tends to see the down side of any situation. Luckily, Nemo and Dory always put a smile on his face.

Slime covering deflects anemone stings

Black-tipped pectoral fin

"WHY DO I KEEP GETTING TALK D INTO INSANE CHOICES?"

TRUE OR FISHY?

Clownfish will chase away human divers if they feel invaded.

True: They bravely defend their homes.

Gloomy gills

When Marlin sees Dory taken safely into the Marine Life Institute, he worries it is a restaurant. Marlin always expects the worst!

17

NEMO

A cute clownfish, Nemo lives with his devoted dad, Marlin, on a beautiful coral reef. Born with one small fin, Nemo is always keen to show his dad he can do anything other fish can do. One of his main tasks in life is to convince Marlin to lighten up and learn to trust others.

Large tail helps add swimming power

Dory danger

Nemo is always concerned about Dory. He is the first to react when she is pulled into the undertow caused by the stringray migration.

Lucky right fin

Nemo's great adventure

On Nemo's first day at school, he was caught by a human diver and taken to live in an aquarium! Dory helped Marlin find him, and now the trio lives together in the coral reef.

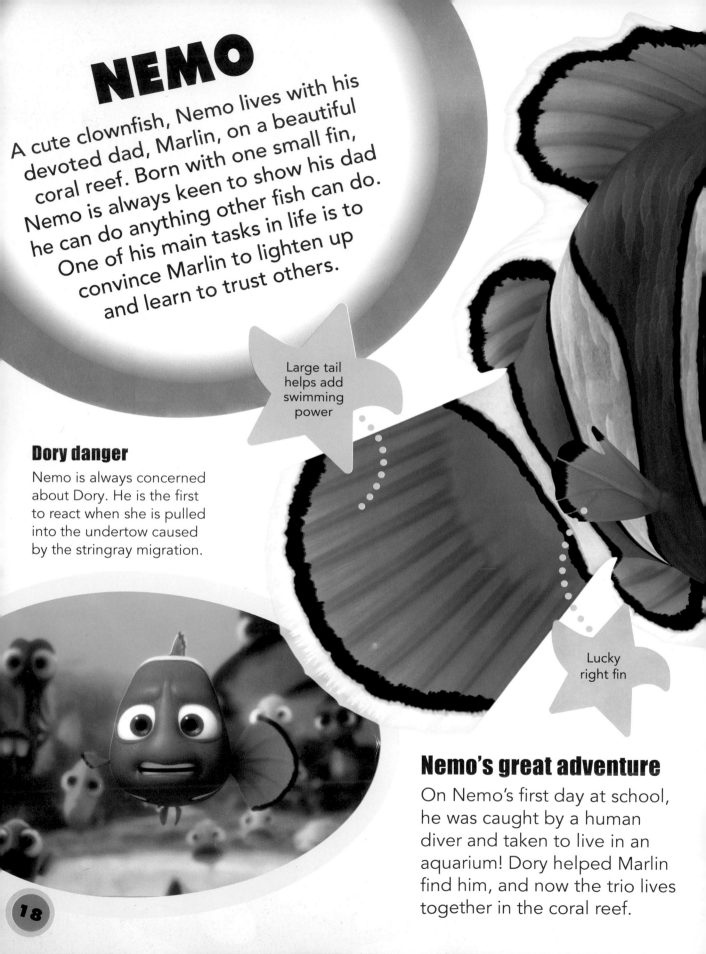

Clownfish have three white stripes

"I MISS DORY."

Minding Dory

Nemo cares deeply about Dory, and knows she can use a little help sometimes. She brings laughter into Nemo's life, and he can't imagine his home without her.

TRUE OR FISHY?

Only clownfish can live inside anemones.

True: No other fish are immune to anemone venom.

Best buddies

An only fish, Nemo has always been very close to his dad. The pair would be lost without each other—and Dory.

19

DISASTER!

NEMO'S BIG IDEA

Important reminder

Guilt trip

Trust issues

Think like Dory

Marlin is refusing to cross the ocean to find Dory's family. He thinks it's too dangerous!

Nemo helps Marlin remember what it felt like to miss his family.

Dory has been taken out of the ocean by MLI staffers. Marlin is nervous about rescuing her.

Nemo reminds Marlin that it was his mean comments to Dory that caused her to swim away in the first place.

Marlin is convinced that their journey in a bucket held by a loon bird will end in disaster.

Nemo tells Marlin that Dory will forget them if they don't reach her quickly.

Marlin and Nemo are trapped in the gift shop pool with no clear way out.

Nemo advises Marlin to be more like Dory. She doesn't think so much—she just does!

AND THE RESULT?

→ Marlin agrees to help Dory. She is their family too, after all.

→ Feelings of guilt and love for Dory push Marlin past his fears. He must find Dory, no matter what!

→ Marlin lets the bird take them to Quarantine. Going by air will have the pair closer to Dory in no time!

→ Marlin and Nemo leap into action, riding on the fountains! Dory would be proud.

DEALING WITH DAD

If anyone can help Dory find her parents, Marlin can. But he is not keen to stray from his safe, familiar life. Luckily, Nemo knows every trick in the book to win over his dad and remind him of his ability to face his fears.

DID YOU KNOW?

Male clownfish are very protective of their eggs. They fan them with their fins to give them oxygen.

MR. RAY

Mr. Ray is more than just a teacher to his pupils at the Sandy Patch School. He is also an explorer of the seas. Full of enthusiasm, Mr. Ray is an inspiring educator who loves to lead his class in song, using catchy tunes to help them remember fascinating facts.

TRUE OR FISHY?

Stingrays like to live near the sea surface where it's warmer.

Fishy: They live on the sand of the sea bed.

Boneless body

White dots camouflage with sandy sea floor

Nemo's class

Mr. Ray is very fond of Nemo's class. It includes a sea horse who is H_2O intolerant and a butterfly fish with a short attention span.

22

Pupil carrier

Transporting pupils on his wings, Mr. Ray knows that his class will always be safe. At the reef he lets them scatter and look around.

Whip-like tail

Words of wisdom

Mr. Ray knows all about following your instincts. He teaches his class that an instinct is "something deep inside you that feels so familiar you have to listen to it—like a song you've always known."

"CLIMB ABOARD, EXPLORERS!"

Class helper

Although she is a keen class assistant, Dory is not always very helpful to Mr. Ray. She has trouble remembering facts and can wander off into trouble on class trips.

Inspiring topic

The stingray migration sounds kind of complicated, but really it's just about the stingrays wanting to go home. It comes from a feeling that Mr. Ray calls an "instinct."

NEMO'S FIELD TRIP

Today Mr. Ray took us on a field trip to see the stringray migration. It was a great day out and we learned lots of things, too. Everyone had fun... Except for Dory who got a bit too close to the action—as you'll see in my report!

Listen to teacher

This is my school gang and me being given safety tips by Mr. Ray. He always tells us to stay away from the reef edge.

Take care!

Poor Dory got too close to the stingrays and was sucked into the undertow. She passed out and Chickenfish asked if she was dead. Some kids thought this was the best bit of the day. She's okay now.

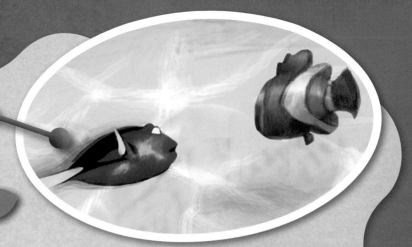

I loved seeing the stingrays go by. They sang even better than Mr. Ray! The sight reminded me of some of my own crazy adventures, traveling across the sea.

Fun ride

I never felt tired on our field trip because Mr. Ray let us all ride everywhere on his back. The water swooshed by and tickled our fins.

All about migration

According to Mr. Ray, migration is "nature's inspiration to move around the sea." My dad says it's better to stay home though.

It's hungry, deadly, and heading their way… What can Dory and her friends do to escape from a giant squid?

HOW TO SURVIVE A SQUID ATTACK

Mantle with small fins at rear

Giant eyes for seeing in dark depths

Hidden beak for shredding flesh

Tentacles have suction cups for clinging to prey

1 KEEP QUIET

If a bunch of crabs tell you to shush, pay attention. They may just happen to know that a giant squid is slumbering nearby—and they wake up mean and hungry.

TRUE OR FISHY?

The giant squid is a mythical beast.

Fishy: Squid can grow to the length of a school bus.

2 SWIM FOR IT

Squid are fast, so you have to be faster. There's no time to lose. Swim as fast as you possibly can!

3 AVOID THE TENTACLES

They may look soft and rubbery, but those tentacles will drag you into the squid's sharp beak. Don't stop to shake hands.

MARINE LIFE
INSTITUTE

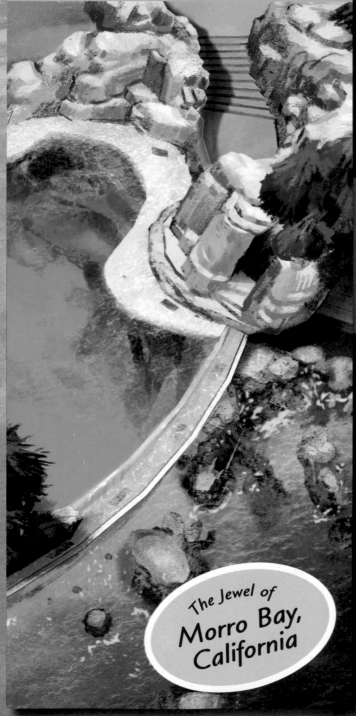

The Jewel of
**Morro Bay,
California**

OUR VISION

Welcome, ocean lover, to the Marine Life Institute. The sea is beautiful, and we can all be part of its magic by learning about, and caring for, its wonderful marine life.

RESCUE

Storms, pollution, sickness, and accidents bring forlorn creatures to our door every day. Our team of marine experts never turns away a sea creature in need.

"Many of our former residents still live locally, like these sea lions, who just love to hang out in beautiful Morro Bay."

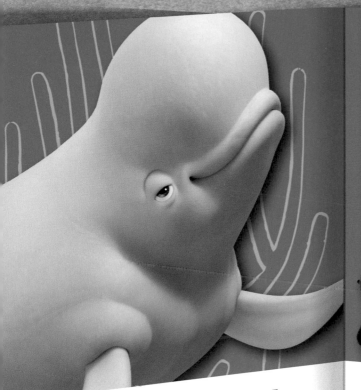

REHABILITATION

Getting well is a gradual process. This is good news for all our human visitors who enjoy returning time after time to see our fascinating ocean friends up close.

RELEASE

Our goal is to release all our sea animals, safe and well, back into their natural ocean habitat. We are sorry to say goodbye, but we take great pride in their recovery.

"Some guys just love being looked after, like Hank, our octopus, who acts like he never wants to leave!"

We love our human visitors. Come again soon!

Known as the jewel of Morro Bay, California, the Marine Life Institute (MLI) is a haven for ocean life. Sea creatures in need are given love and care in a series of perfectly simulated marine environments—and are gazed at by a fascinated public.

OPEN OCEAN

KID ZONE

Open Ocean exhibit, with a stunning colorful, cylindrical tank

TIDAL TRAIL

Main containment pool zone —marine life central

Gift shop

Everyone's favorite stop, the gift shop sells everything ocean-related you could wish for— except live fish. Toy clownfish are always big sellers here.

Open Ocean

This awe-inspiring zone recreates the wonders of the deep, with the bright colors of the reef and hundreds of different types of fish.

Exterior whale pools—a real showstopper!

WHALE SHARK

MARINE LIFE INSTITUTE

Parking and drop-off for humans

JELLYFISH JUNGLE

JOURNEY TO THE DEEP

TIDAL TRAIL

NEPTUNES SOUNDS OF THE DEEP

BELUGA

Rehab zones for those heading back to sea

Touch pool

The hands are coming! This touchy-feely zone is great fun for kids, but can be a little disturbing for the sensitive sea life getting handled here.

Pipe room

Even for a savvy octopus like Hank, the MLI pipe room is a bit of a maze. And frankly, Dory isn't the ideal companion for remembering directions!

Whale pool

The perfect place to get a new angle on the sea's biggest attractions. Those who speak whale can even hear Destiny and Bailey chatting.

HANK

This grouchy octopus is actually a septopus—he lost one arm! All Hank wants is to be moved to a cozy aquarium in Cleveland, but Dory helps him see that life isn't only about helping yourself. At last, Hank has a reason to put his skills as a master of disguise into action.

Wanting out

When Hank first meets Dory in Quarantine, he sees her as his ticket to stay out of the ocean forever. He agrees to help her find her parents, in exchange for her sick tag.

Hank hangs on

Hank is not always in control. He has to rely on Dory to lead him to safety, away from the horrors of the touch pool.

Suction cups for sticking to things

TRUE OR FISHY?

An octopus often gets tangled up in its own tentacles.

Fishy: Special sensors prevent this from happening.

Driving Dory

All those arms come in handy when Dory gives Hank his biggest challenge yet—driving a truck full of sea creatures!

DID YOU KNOW?

The octopus is intelligent. It has a long-term and short-term memory, can use tools, and can solve problems.

Keen eyesight aids survival

"NEWS FLASH— NOBODY'S FINE!"

Skin can change color and texture

All heart

A tough life has made Hank a seriously sulky guy. When Dory arrives, she brings friendship into his life and reminds him that someone with three hearts really ought to be a bit nicer.

SNEAKY SEPTOPUS

If you are trying to sneak around a building then there is no better helper than Hank. He is a whiz at hiding, creeping, and crawling away from those who want to send him back into the ocean. Watch the master at work!

Know your enemy

Hank waits until staffers are busy before making his move. He knows that once a human gets on the phone, they can chat for hours.

Master of improvisation

Hank needs something to carry Dory in, so he uses a handy carafe. Of course, he had to drink the coffee first to empty it.

Blending in

Hank is not just an expert at marine camouflage. He can also blend in among the man-made features of the MLI. He's almost impossible to spot!

Keep them peeled

Never taking anything for granted, Hank always takes a final peek at the lay of the land before he breaks cover.

Local knowledge

Hank takes Dory straight to the map in the staff office. Sneaking around is much more effective if you don't waste time getting lost.

Aquatic acrobat

It takes the skill of a gymnast to travel across large rooms without being seen. Luckily there are pipes everywhere to climb and swing on.

Play acting

Hank is great at play-acting. He can become a baby or a child's toy at will. Dory isn't as good as Hank, and is far too chatty to play dead in the bait bucket.

Spot an opportunity

Dory can be pretty sneaky too! She dives into a bucket that she thinks is her destiny. The fish in there are strangely quiet....

SEA LIONS

Fluke and Rudder are two lazy sea lions who spend all day loafing around on the sunny rocks near the MLI. The one activity that gets these two laid-back buddies excited is keeping their neighbor, Gerald, off their favorite basking space. Off! Off! Off!

Ear flap

Bushy unibrow

Friendly favor

Gerald has one thing going for him—he's the owner of a bucket that he will lend out, in exchange for a turn on the rock.

Gerald

Long foreflipper

"WE'RE TRYING TO SLEEP!"

Rescued and released

As former residents, Fluke and Rudder know the MLI well. Now that they're fixed up, they are ready to do… as little as possible! If only Gerald would shove off and leave them to nap!

Short, thick fur

Helping hand

Sympathetic Fluke and Rudder are happy to help Marlin and Nemo get inside the MLI. They call on their friend Becky the loon bird to lend a helping wing.

Whiskers sense movement in water

TRUE OR FISHY?

Sea lions can breathe under water.

Fishy: They have to hold their breath when diving.

Rudder

Fluke

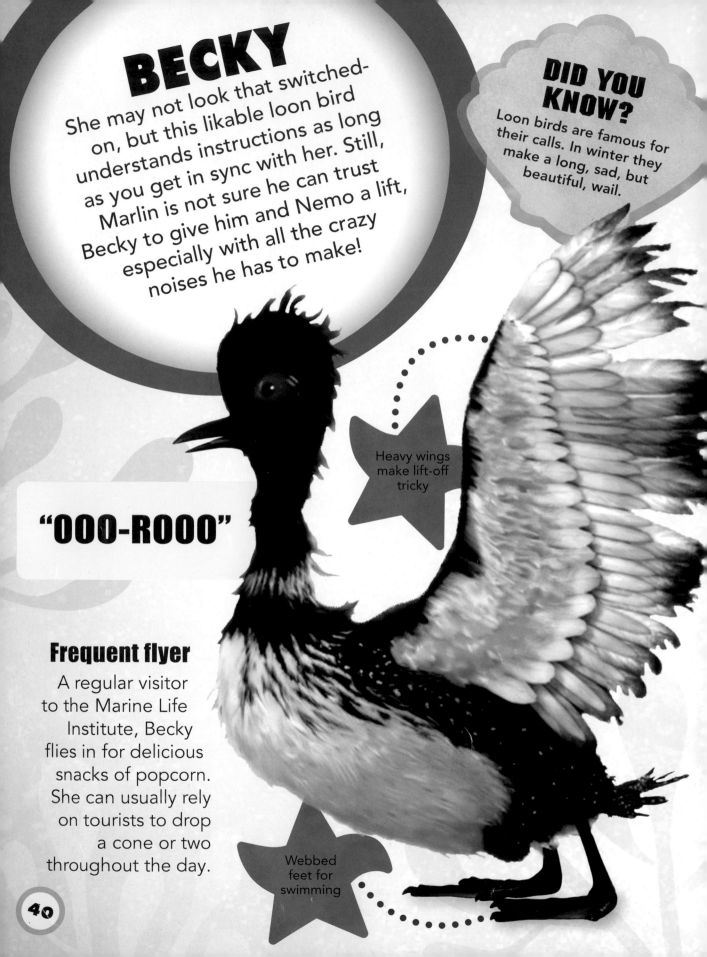

BECKY

She may not look that switched-on, but this likable loon bird understands instructions as long as you get in sync with her. Still, Marlin is not sure he can trust Becky to give him and Nemo a lift, especially with all the crazy noises he has to make!

DID YOU KNOW?

Loon birds are famous for their calls. In winter they make a long, sad, but beautiful, wail.

"OOO-ROOO"

Heavy wings make lift-off tricky

Frequent flyer

A regular visitor to the Marine Life Institute, Becky flies in for delicious snacks of popcorn. She can usually rely on tourists to drop a cone or two throughout the day.

Webbed feet for swimming

Getting pecky

Marlin is not thrilled when he finds out Becky will be giving him a lift. She keeps pecking him!

Tuning in

The only way to get through to Becky is to imprint yourself on her by making loon noises and staring her in the eye. After that, she'll never forget you.

TRUE OR FISHY?

Loon birds regularly eat small stones.

True: It sounds loony, but the stones help with digestion.

Feathered friend

Becky is a friend to Fluke and Rudder. She helps them out if they ask her very politely.

DORY'S HOME

A warm sea, a coral cave, soft sea grass, and squishy sand—Dory's childhood home was a wonderful place to grow up. Yet her home was not actually in the real ocean—something that she was only to recall a long time later.

Water temperature kept at 75 to 77°F

Colorful butterfly fish

Home sweet home

Dory loved her childhood cave, but often forgot the way to it. Later, finding her way home takes her on the adventure of her life!

TRUE OR FISHY?

Blue tang fish like Dory are born yellow.

Answer: Amazingly true!

Safe from harm

Unlike some fish, Dory grew up where all fish were friends. No hungry predators came hunting for the blue tangs—they were all safe and sound in an aquarium.

Stripy angelfish

Man-made reef with living coral

The open ocean?

Dory's home was not out at sea. Instead it was in a man-made enclosure called the Open Ocean exhibit at the Marine Life Institute.

DESTINY

One of the stars of the MLI, Destiny is a whale shark who was rescued after her poor eyesight meant she became a nervous swimmer. She and Dory go way back. The two friends used to chat through the pipes in their pools. Dory loved hearing Destiny's funny stories again and again.

DID YOU KNOW?
The whale shark's only known predator is the human.

Unique personal spot pattern

Thick, protective skin

Bailey's buddy

Destiny is never short of someone to talk to with Bailey in the pool next door. They know each other well enough to put up with a little playful banter.

Pool home

Destiny has a state-of-the-art pool to swim in, but with her poor eyesight she has trouble avoiding crashing into the walls.

"WE WERE PIPE PALS!"

Very wide mouth

A new destiny

A little support from her friends is all Destiny needs to return to the wild. She is worried about bumping into things, but her good friends offer to be her eyes as she makes her leap to freedom.

TRUE OR FISHY?

Whale sharks are the largest living fish on the planet.

True: Bigger sea creatures are mammals, not fish.

45

BAILEY

Bailey is a rescued beluga whale, now attracting crowds to the MLI. He suffered a blow to the head in the wild, which he believes gave him a swollen head and affected his ability to echolocate. He never stops worrying about his injury. But, in fact, all belugas look like him!

White skin for camouflage in ice

Flippers have rounded edges

Whale wail

Even though the doctors say Bailey is okay now, he doesn't believe them. He often complains of headaches and does not like others talking about his injury.

DID YOU KNOW?

The beluga whale is actually born dark gray. It takes years for it to change into its well-known white color.

TRUE OR FISHY?

Belugas are so fond of singing they are known as sea canaries.

True: They can produce whistling and chirping sounds.

46

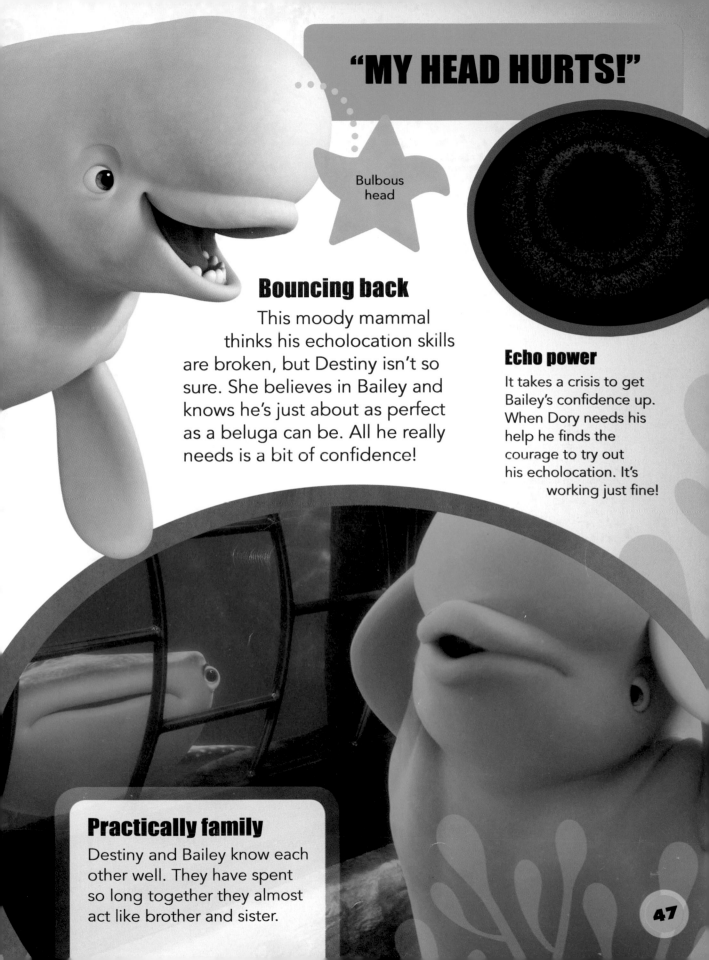

"MY HEAD HURTS!"

Bulbous head

Bouncing back

This moody mammal thinks his echolocation skills are broken, but Destiny isn't so sure. She believes in Bailey and knows he's just about as perfect as a beluga can be. All he really needs is a bit of confidence!

Echo power

It takes a crisis to get Bailey's confidence up. When Dory needs his help he finds the courage to try out his echolocation. It's working just fine!

Practically family

Destiny and Bailey know each other well. They have spent so long together they almost act like brother and sister.

Bailey the beluga whale has the amazing ability of echolocation, which allows him to see things that others can't. Bailey is convinced that a head injury stopped his skills from developing. It is up to his pals at the MLI to prove him wrong.

Seeing in the dark

Bailey's echolocation is the perfect solution when Dory is lost in the pipes of the MLI. She really needs someone who can see around corners, and Bailey is the mammal for the job.

WITNESS THE WORLD'S MOST

LOCATION

Belugas send out a fast clicking sound through their bulbous heads. The echoes that bounce back give the whales a picture of everything around them.

All in the mind

It's all a matter of confidence—as soon as Bailey believes in his power, it comes rushing in!

WERFUL PAIR OF GLASSES

TOUCH POOL TERROR

For the children who visit the MLI, this pool is a treat—it is the place where they can pick up, pet, and play with the sea creatures that they love. For the marine critters themselves, it is a very different story!

Urchin's leathery outer skin

Poker's cove

The worst part of the touch pool is Poker's Cove. This is the perfect spot for kids to reach in and get grabby. The poor starfish hate being pulled and stretched.

Hands of doom

At first Dory thinks that the inhabitants of the pool are telling her about someone called Hans... Then she realizes the awful truth—the hands are coming! Watch out!

Curious human finger pokes urchin

Escape

Hank thinks Dory is crazy to break cover, but she knows if she just keeps swimming, she'll get him out. Which is good, as she got him in there in the first place!

Dirty water

Hank is so frightened by Poker's Cove that he has an inky accident. It turns the entire pool black... As well as some poking fingers!

Tube feet aid urchin's movement

SHELLFISH

Shellfish of all shapes and sizes lurk everywhere in the ocean, so Dory is always bumping into them. Some may be crabby customers, but most will usually help those in need of news or directions. After all, nobody likes a selfish shellfish!

Pearl sits inside clam

Big-mouthed clam

This lonely chatterbox clam is desperate to talk to Marlin and Nemo—or anyone really—about his love life. Why did his girl Shelley leave him?

Both shells are equally sized

"I HAVEN'T HAD ANYONE TO TALK TO IN YEARS." CLAM

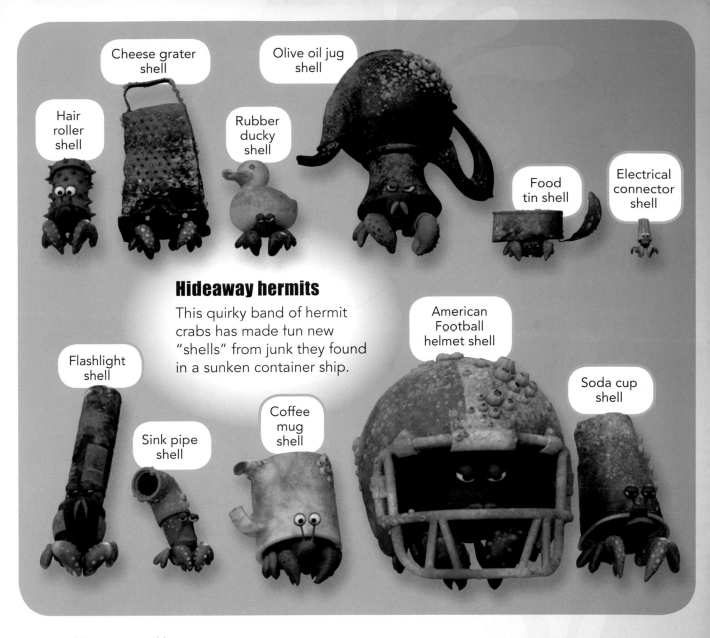

Hair roller shell

Cheese grater shell

Olive oil jug shell

Rubber ducky shell

Food tin shell

Electrical connector shell

Hideaway hermits

This quirky band of hermit crabs has made fun new "shells" from junk they found in a sunken container ship.

Flashlight shell

American Football helmet shell

Sink pipe shell

Coffee mug shell

Soda cup shell

Crabs next door

These miniature crabs live in the Open Ocean exhibit with the blue tangs. They know all about the tangs' comings and goings—luckily for Dory.

TRUE OR FISHY?

Crabs grow new shells and have to climb out of their old ones.

True: They moult often as they get older.

DISLIKES:
Predators, including sharks and orcas.

FAVORITE FOOD:
Fish and crabs.

LIKES:
Swimming, hugging, and being photographed.

OTTER

JOIN THE CUDDLE

CUTE FACT: Otters make and play on their own water slides.

CUTE FACT: Otters sometimes hold hands while they nap so they aren't separated.

CUTENESS PARTY

Endless possibilities

Living out at sea you never know what each new day will bring. It is wild out there—but that is half of the fun.

Finny friends

There are so many creatures in the sea, you can make a new friend every single day. The only trouble is remembering their names!

OUT

Life in the ocean is filled with infinite wonder and endless adventure. At least that is what Dory says.

Dory wants to return to a life at sea with her family—that's where it's all happening!

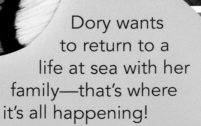

Spectacular sights

Only in the wild can you see awesome events of nature, such as the amazing stingray migration. That wouldn't happen in a tank!

Hank has extremely unhappy memories of the ocean. He is much happier in captivity.

OR **IN?**

Hank thinks a safe place of healing is perfect for the quiet life. What could be better than life on the inside?

Top healthcare

With the very latest scientific research put into practice, the MLI has the best facilities for keeping its occupants safe and well.

Safe from harm

With the big eaters safely contained in their own pools, there is no chance that you will end up on the lunch menu here.

Personal touch

The highly trained staff at the MLI will come running to help you at the first sign of a drooping fin. It's like being in a five-star fish hotel!

Jenny and Charlie
(Mom and Dad)

Species: Blue tangs

Blue with yellow fins,
just like Dory!

Jenny is very wise and
Charlie is a real joker.

These loving parents
totally adore Dory.

Nemo

Species: Clownfish

Small with orange-and-white
stripes and a little fin
on one side.

Cheerful, funny, and sweet.

Always tries to fight Dory's
corner with Marlin.

Hank

Species: Octopus.

Orange and squishy
with seven arms.

Helpful guy,
but rather grouchy.

He is pretty happy
being unhappy.

WHO'S WHO?

There are many friends
and family members in Dory's life
now. She may be a forgetful fish,
but she always tries her best
to remember the most
important things about
each familiar face.

Bailey

Species: Beluga whale

Big guy with kind of
a melon head.

Makes a strange but cool
sound when he echolocates.

Moody, but deep down,
he is a good guy.

Destiny

Species: Whale shark

Spotty with a great
big smile.

Dory's best friend from
way back.

Has bad eyesight—keeps
bumping into things.

Mr. Ray

Species: Stingray

Dark blue with big wings
for riding on.

Teacher, singer, and
school bus!

Lets Dory help out
with his class.

Marlin

Species: Clownfish

Orange and white
like Nemo—only bigger.

Worries about Dory a lot.

Used to be Mr. Grumpy
Gills. Now he's much
more cheery.

WHAT WOULD DORY DO?

Dory has a never-give-up spirit and tons of crazy ideas. Without even realizing it, she has become an inspiration to those around her. Everyone can learn from her words of wisdom.

WHAT IS SO GREAT ABOUT **PLANS?** I'VE NEVER HAD A PLAN.

JUST TRY SOMETHING!

JUST KEEP SWIMMING.

I KNOW YOU'RE SCARED, BUT YOU CAN'T GIVE UP. FOLLOW ME!

I CAN FIX IT!

I'M OKAY WITH CRAZY.

THERE'S GOT TO BE A WAY. THERE'S ALWAYS A WAY.

Crazy climax

It's Dory's unique attitude that gets her friends rescued. Who else could help them escape from the back of a moving truck?

After meeting Dory's gang of extraordinary friends, her parents are happy to relocate to the coral reef. They would follow her anywhere.

GOING HOME

From the tiniest plankton in the sea to the stingrays of the great migration, every sea creature feels the deep call for home. Through many crazy adventures, these friends have come to realize where they truly belong.

MR. HANK

Hank is ready to follow Dory back to the big blue ocean. However, taking over Mr. Ray's class while he is on migration may be more excitement than Hank needs!

STAYING TOGETHER

UNFORGETTABLE

Marlin and Nemo should have guessed that Dory would never leave them behind. Now both her old and new families fit together to make one big one.

Now Dory gets to live with her favorite clownfish, her parents, a septopus, two whales, and a whole host of neighbors. She has finally found a home that is definitely unforgettable!

ACKNOWLEDGMENTS

Project Editor Lisa Stock
Additional Editors Elizabeth Dowsett and Lauren Nesworthy
Senior Designer Lynne Moulding
Additional Designers Chris Gould and Anna Pond
Pre-Production Producer Marc Staples
Senior Producer Alex Bell
Managing Editor Sadie Smith
Design Manager Ron Stobbart
Publisher Julie Ferris
Art Director Lisa Lanzarini
Publishing Director Simon Beecroft

First American Edition, 2016
Published in the United States by DK Publishing
345 Hudson Street, New York, New York 10014

Page design copyright © 2016 Dorling Kindersley Limited
DK, a Division of Penguin Random House LLC

16 17 18 19   10 9 8 7 6 5 4 3 2 1
001–259539–05/16

A catalog record for this book is available
from the Library of Congress.

ISBN: 978-1-4654-4978-8

DK books are available at special discounts when purchased in
bulk for sales promotions, premiums, fund-raising, or
educational use. For details, contact: DK Publishing Special
Markets, 345 Hudson Street, New York, New York 10014
SpecialSales@dk.com

Printed and bound in the USA.

A WORLD OF IDEAS
SEE ALL THERE IS TO KNOW

Discover more at
www.dk.com
www.disney.com
www.pixar.com